# ELEMENTS OF TEACHER EFFECTIVENESS

# Rewarding Excellence
## Teacher Evaluation and Compensation

Cheryl C. Sullivan

National School Boards Association
Alexandria, Virginia

ISBN 0-88364-251-4

National School Boards Association
1680 Duke Street
Alexandria, VA 223124

# Contents

# Foreword

T he quality of America's teachers will determine whether our nation successfully raises academic achievement so that all students will be educationally prepared for life in the 21st century. The policies and strategies adopted by local school boards will go a long way in determining how effective individual school systems will be in providing the teaching force their students need. Part of that school board role involves the strategic alignment of classroom teaching with the high standards and accountability needed for academic success. To assist local boards, NSBA has developed the Key Work of School Boards initiative, which provides board members with a policy-making process and the content knowledge they need to support their governance role in raising student achievement—including board action to develop and inspire effective teaching.

*Rewarding Excellence: Teacher Evaluation and Compensation* is the second publication in NSBA's series, Elements of Teacher Effectiveness. This report examines the crucial role that teacher evaluation and compensation programs play in attaining goals for high-quality teaching. Specifically, the report reviews major studies, identifies various common practices that do not encourage or help teachers, and offers recommendations that are supported by on-going research in this important area.

The first report in this series, *Into the Classroom*, reviews the research and makes recommendations for local policy makers regarding the recruitment, preparation, and licensure of teachers. The next report will follow a similar course in the area of professional development.

After reading *Rewarding Excellence*, education policy makers and administrators at all levels are likely to view current evaluation and compensation practices with a more strategic eye and know that there are alternatives available that merit their consideration.


Anne L. Bryant
Executive Director

# Acknowledgments

T his report has benefited from the contributions of many. Michael A. Resnick, associate executive director of NSBA, reviewed several drafts and provided general oversight of the project. Dan Goldhaber, principal research associate at the Urban Institute; Michael Podgursky, professor and chairman of the economics department at the University of Missouri; and Richard Murnane Thompson, professor of education and society at the Harvard Graduate School of Education, provided comments and suggestions that contributed immensely to the report's clarity, tone, and balance. Drew Lindsay, an independent editor, edited the prepublication draft. Sally Zakariya, NSBA's publications director, coordinated the production of the report (and series), and Laurie Juliana, an independent editor, helped put the manuscript into final form.

# Executive Summary

R ecent studies documenting the importance of effective teaching have led
policy makers at all levels of government to begin exploring new
approaches to teacher evaluation and compensation. During much of the
20th century, little changed in the methods by which teachers were
evaluated and paid. But in recent years, a host of promising new ideas have
been proposed—and with them, new questions and challenges have emerged.

*Rewarding Excellence*, the second report in NSBA's series on teacher
effectiveness, opens with a critical analysis of teacher-evaluation methods in use
today—including observations by principals, student and parent appraisals, and
peer reviews—and argues that, in isolation, such subjective measures cannot
accurately assess a teacher's contribution to student learning. Next, the report
examines objective teacher-evaluation measures that are directly linked to student
achievement. States and districts are currently building such measures into new
accountability systems based on standardized tests, and—while none of these
systems is perfect—they promise a much more accurate picture of teacher quality
than has previously existed. Value-added systems (that is, accountability systems
that focus on the value added to student performance by the school or teacher),
such as those used in Tennessee and Dallas, are helping officials more accurately
assess teachers' contributions to student learning.

*Rewarding Excellence* goes on to tackle the complicated and controversial
topic of teacher compensation, arguing that salary systems must offer incentives
for teachers to increase student achievement. According to the report, the
single-salary structure so prevalent in school districts across America, as well as
recent experiments in teacher compensation—including merit-pay plans and
portfolios—all lack adequate incentives. The report examines compensation
systems based on the acquisition of skills—including those measured by the
National Board for Professional Teaching Standards (NBPTS)—concluding that
they, too, suffer deficiencies and lack evidence demonstrating their effectiveness.
Clearly, dramatic changes are needed, with a focus on revamping salary systems
to link teachers' pay to how well their students learn.

*Rewarding Excellence* offers a number of conclusions and recommendations
that underscore the importance of aligning evaluation and compensation with
student performance. In the area of teacher evaluation, the report urges school
districts to give serious consideration to the adoption of systems based on
value-added assessments, coupled with written reviews from peers, principals,
parents, and students. It also recommends that districts and states consider
linking pay systems directly to teachers' performance as measured by gains in
student learning. The report concludes with suggestions about how to build such
pay-for-performance systems, posing several key questions that school boards
should consider.

# Introduction

eachers' salaries represent the single largest expenditure in most school districts' budgets, and for that reason, it is surprising that alternative strategies for evaluating and compensating teachers have attracted so little attention from education reformers. For much of the 20th century, there was little question as to how teachers were to be evaluated and compensated. Indeed, many questioned whether tenured teachers needed to be evaluated at all, since much of the curriculum was considered "teacher proof," implying that anyone could teach it effectively.[1] If a teacher's performance was judged, it was often done casually by the school principal, who would observe one or more classes and check off items on a list of required demonstrated skills.

Teachers' pay was decided in a similarly perfunctory way that based salary on level of educational attainment and years in the classroom. The single-salary schedule was introduced in an effort to professionalize teaching and end the cronyism that based salaries and career opportunities on political connections. In particular, reformers reacted against existing disparities in pay for women and minorities, implementing the single-salary schedule to better reflect the principle of horizontal equity.

More recently, as the quality of teachers has emerged as an issue of paramount importance to improving student achievement, some school reformers have begun to lobby against the status quo on teacher evaluation and pay. Historically, administrators and policy makers have been reluctant to initiate such change because of the political volatility of the issue.[2] But after the 1983 publication of *A Nation at Risk*,[3] some schools began to experiment with peer review, observations by principals, and teacher portfolios. In 1987, a nonprofit group called the National Board for Professional Teaching Standards (NBPTS) was created in an attempt to develop, as part of an advanced certification process, a national teacher evaluation system that would avoid the perceived biases of evaluations by peers and principals (see "Competency- and Skill-Based Pay," page 11).

Such initiatives have focused attention on the need to evaluate teachers and modernize an anachronistic pay system. But many of the new methods of evaluation and compensation have yielded unreliable data about teaching quality, and others have yet to prove they will boost student achievement. In the end,

1

reformers and administrators will have to discard long-standing assumptions about teacher quality if they are to build evaluation and compensation systems that will directly contribute to student achievement.

Aside from this introduction and a concluding section that proposes several policy recommendations, this report is divided into two parts. Part I examines the issue of teacher evaluation, focusing on the importance of developing accountability systems that include both student achievement outcomes and subjective evaluations of teacher effectiveness. In Part II, various approaches to teacher compensation are examined, including the single-salary schedule, merit pay, portfolios, and competency- and skill-based pay, as well as programs that tie teacher pay more directly to student performance.

# Part I:
# Teacher Evaluation

A s citizens demand greater productivity from America's public schools, attention has focused increasingly on how teachers are evaluated and the degree to which various approaches are aligned with student achievement objectives. This section discusses the current state of teacher evaluation procedures and explores several alternatives to existing systems. (See Appendix A for a comparison of approaches to teacher evaluation.)

## SUBJECTIVE TEACHER EVALUATIONS

The most common tool for evaluating teachers today is evaluation by the school principal. In fact, one study found that 99.8 percent of public schools use the principals' classroom observations as the primary source of data for teacher evaluations.[4] This approach can provide valuable information on teachers' instructional style, teacher-student interactions, and classroom environment.[5] However, making evaluations by principals the sole indicator of teacher performance can be problematic. Often, such evaluations are based on only a few observations (usually one), and because the presence of the principal can change the behavior of both students and teachers, these evaluations rarely capture the true classroom environment.[6] Also, given the difficulty in firing tenured teachers, principals have little incentive to give evaluations that are less than favorable. Candid school administrators might well find themselves in the awkward position of having to work with teachers to whom they have given poor ratings. It is not surprising, then, that research shows that principals' judgments are often inflated and that this type of assessment has had little impact on teacher performance.[7]

Many scholars have advocated "360-degree" assessments, which supplement evaluation by the principal with self-assessments and feedback from peers, parents, and students. A number of school districts have experimented with such assessments, either wholly or in part, to gain a more complete picture of teacher performance. For example, the Douglas County School District (in Colorado), the Virginia Beach City Public Schools (in Virginia), and the Williamsburg-James City Public Schools (also in Virginia) use student and/or parent evaluations, while the Lenawee Intermediate School District (in Michigan) employs peer evaluations.[8]

## Student Evaluations

A number of scholars have indicated that evaluations from students are the most valid and reliable indicator of teacher performance.[9] One particular study found no significant differences between students' ratings of teachers and those of a qualified expert.[10] Furthermore, research has shown a positive relationship between the use of student ratings and increased student learning.[11]

## Parent Evaluations

Several studies have found that teachers value parents' feedback as credible information that can be used to improve performance.[12] Indeed, one study indicated that teachers advocated the use of parent evaluations in making merit-pay decisions,[13] and another found that at least some parents may know more about certain aspects of teacher quality than other evaluators do. In a study of teacher evaluations, Epstein concluded, "[Parents] may be knowledgeable about how the teacher interacts with the child and family, responds to the student's needs and skills, assigns appropriate challenges in books and in homework, and inspires the student to continue commitment to school work at home—all indicators of effective teaching."[14]

## Peer Evaluations

Although there are limitations to peer evaluations—such as lack of direct knowledge of another teacher's performance and possible conflict of interest—they can provide valuable feedback to teachers, especially if implemented properly.[15] For example, peer evaluations should be completed only by colleagues who have direct knowledge of the teacher's performance, such as a reading specialist who has worked with the teacher or another teacher in the same discipline or grade level who has collaborated with the teacher who is being evaluated.

Many observers see the 360-degree approach to teacher evaluation as an improvement over evaluations based on principals' observations alone. They argue that student, parent, and peer evaluations can provide critical information that principals may not always be in a position to collect. Yet this approach is weakened due to its reliance on subjective measures that may suffer from the same inherent biases and prejudices as evaluations by principals. Moreover, 360-degree assessments do not provide a direct, concrete measure of teachers' contributions to student learning.

# OBJECTIVE EVALUATIONS

The growing movement to increase accountability within school systems has motivated many districts and states to adopt outcome-oriented measures of teacher quality to supplement less direct measures, such as evaluations by principals and 360-degree assessments. One approach has been to take gains

4

in student learning as a measure of teachers' performance in the classroom. As the Education Commission of the States reported: "Regardless of credentials, regardless of experience, regardless of supervisors' prior evaluations, what really matters—what really proves if a teacher is doing his or her job—is whether students are learning."[16]

Using this philosophy, states and districts have built accountability programs to hold teachers and administrators responsible for students' progress toward predetermined educational standards. Still, some educators—especially teachers— worry that these new forms of accountability are misleading as well as destructive to the educational climate. Standardized tests, they say, cannot measure higher-order analytical skills and cannot accurately assess student knowledge due to their limited coverage of the material taught in the classroom.[17] Others warn against the potential unanticipated consequences of poorly structured teacher evaluation systems. For instance, some fear that accountability systems based on such tests will lead to cheating, teaching to the test, and a narrowing of the curriculum.[18]

Still other critics argue that standardized tests are a poor yardstick by which to judge teacher performance. Teachers, for example, have no control over key variables—including a student's socioeconomic status, language proficiency, and home and peer influences—that affect achievement. Team teaching, pull-out programs, and instructional aides also blur the assessment of a teacher's contribution to student achievement.

---

*"Many observers see the 360-degree approach to teacher evaluation as an improvement over evaluations based on principals' observations alone."*

---

Many of these perceived weaknesses relate specifically to the use of average test scores in accountability systems. As Robert Meyers notes, the use of average test scores can present insurmountable problems of interpretation:

Average test scores are biased against schools that serve disproportionately higher numbers of academically disadvantaged students because they are influenced by factors other than school performance (for example, student achievement prior to entering first grade, as well as student, family, and community characteristics).

Average test scores reflect out-of-date school performance information. For example, while average test scores for a group of 10th-grade students might be used to assess the performance of their current teacher, they actually reflect learning that occurred from kindergarten through 10th grade.

Average test scores at the school, district, and state levels tend not to be good measures because of student mobility in and out of different schools.

Average test scores do not yield data on a specific classroom or grade level—the natural unit of accountability in schools.[19]

A number of states and districts have addressed the limitations of standardized test scores by building accountability systems that focus on the value added to student performance by the school or teacher. These more sophisticated systems employ advanced statistical techniques to separate out nonschool effects from those that can be attributed to the school environment. Unlike accountability systems that rely on average test scores, these systems track the achievement of individual students from year to year. When such systems are based on data averaged over several years rather than a single year, they can provide reliable data that analysts can use to study the performance of individual teachers, grades, and schools.[20]

## Value-Added Assessment Systems

The two most prominent value-added assessment initiatives are the Dallas Independent School District Value-Assessment Program and the Tennessee Value-Added Assessment System. Other states (for example, South Carolina) and districts also use value-added assessments to increase teacher effectiveness, and Florida has plans to introduce such a system in the near future.

The Dallas Independent School District implemented its value-added evaluation system as a means of assessing teacher performance and determining weaknesses in the school system.[21] District officials established straightforward and student-oriented goals for the new evaluation system, including the improvement of classroom instruction based on student outcomes.[22] Under the approach used in Dallas, the contribution that teachers make to the learning process is determined by factoring out the influence of student background variables (gender, ethnicity, language proficiency, and socioeconomic status, which account for 9 percent to 20 percent of student achievement variance), and school-level variables that are beyond the control of school administrators and teachers (overcrowded conditions in schools, mobility rates, and so on).[23]

The Tennessee Value-Added Assessment System provides data based on a statistical approach that differs significantly from that used in the Dallas program.[24] While the latter controls directly for student background factors, the approach used in Tennessee relies on less direct measures of nonschool-related factors. In the Tennessee model, each individual child is tracked and evaluated every year from the time the student enters school until he graduates or leaves the state. This model controls for external factors by taking a baseline score in the first year the child enters school and then measures that child's progress each subsequent year by comparing prior-year test scores to current-year test scores. This value-added assessment system assumes that the student's external influences will remain constant from year to year, hypothetically making it unnecessary to control directly for outside factors. Although William Sanders, the developer of the Tennessee model, has asserted that his model totally controls for differences in children's backgrounds, recent research has indicated that this model may be fallible.[25] Until the validity of Sanders' approach can be determined, districts would be wise to implement evaluation systems that control directly for student background characteristics.

Methodological differences aside, data analyses of both the Dallas and Tennessee programs suggest that the most important factor in students' academic growth is teacher effectiveness. Drawing on many years of data, Sanders and Sandra Horn concluded that "improvement of student learning must begin with the improvement of relatively ineffective teachers."[26] Tennessee's value-added assessment system identifies teachers who may need additional professional development, mentoring, or other resources to become more competent teachers, a crucial step in increasing teacher quality.

Perhaps the biggest benefit of value-added assessment systems such as those in Dallas and Tennessee is that they provide objective measures of teacher outcomes. As James Stronge argues, "a comprehensive teacher evaluation system ... should be *outcome oriented*, contributing to the personal goals of the teacher and to the mission of the program, the school, and the total educational organization."[27]

As states and school districts begin to gain an appreciation of just how inefficient current evaluation systems are, and as they investigate how to create data-driven systems to raise performance, value-added systems of accountability are likely to become more prevalent. Even in those states that do not mandate testing of students every year, districts often administer annual assessment programs of their own, using tests such as the SAT9 or ITBS. Yet few districts attempt to link test records and examine patterns of student achievement gains over time, much less apply sophisticated statistical techniques to produce value-added scores. With appropriate funding, however, movement in this direction may well produce a sea change in public education like none seen before.

## Multiple Measures

Higher test scores reflect only one of many valued outcomes of public education. A teacher may inspire a student with low self-esteem to reach for higher goals, help a child develop a greater sense of civic responsibility, or even contribute significantly to a school's racial climate with little immediate or direct impact on student's test-score performance. Officials in Dallas and Tennessee acknowledge that value-added assessments alone are not able to fully capture the overall performance of individual teachers. In Dallas, value-added assessments are supplemented by parent, peer, and community member assessments as well as student appraisals. Portfolios and interviews are used occasionally, too, most often when teachers are rated below average on other measures. And, in Tennessee, the state legislature mandated that teachers could not be evaluated solely on the basis of data provided through value-added assessments, opening the door to the use of other measures of effectiveness.

The growing body of research on value-added assessments and 360-degree evaluations suggests that teacher performance should be measured by a variety of outcome measures. The potential advantages of using multiple sources of data for teacher evaluation include:

- A more complete picture of teachers' performance

- Use of both primary and secondary data sources (for example, teacher's self-assessments and student test scores)

- Greater reliability in the documentation of teacher performance

- Greater objectivity in measuring performance

- Documentation of teachers' performance that is closely related to their work in the classroom.[28]

In combination, value-added assessments and 360-degree evaluations may offer a better means of measuring teacher quality than traditional principal observations alone. Value-added assessments give constructive feedback on objective variables, while controlling for outside factors, and 360-degree evaluations provide useful information on teacher performance that cannot be evaluated by student test scores alone. But the development of more comprehensive evaluation systems of this type will require the commitment and participation of school boards, teachers, teachers' unions, administrators, parents, and students alike. Indeed, in districts like Colorado's Douglas County, where some aspects of this approach have been implemented, stakeholders (including the teachers' unions) were actively involved at every stage in the process. Finally, school districts adopting multiple measures of effectiveness must ultimately determine the relative weights attached to each measure—an important feature of such systems, since the choice of weights is likely to have a major impact on the distribution of rewards.

# Part II:
# Teacher Compensation

I n large part, whether or not new teacher evaluation systems pay off in higher student achievement will be determined by the degree to which teacher performance is linked to teacher compensation. This section contrasts the existing single-salary approach to teacher compensation with recent experimental programs that more closely align teacher pay with student outcomes, including merit pay, portfolios, competency- and skill-based pay, and programs that tie teacher pay to student performance (see Appendix B for a comparison of the principal features of these approaches).[29]

## SINGLE-SALARY SCHEDULE

When first implemented in the early 20th century, the single-salary schedule was considered the best approach to teacher compensation. It allotted pay increases based on a teacher's years of experience, units of study completed, and educational degrees.[30] Historically, teachers' unions have been successful in defending the single-salary schedule as both fair and equitable, arguing that it guards against favoritism and gives different teachers the same amount of pay for the same amount of work. But the nature of teaching has changed considerably since the beginning of the century, and a number of education reformers have called for a corresponding change in teacher compensation.

There are at least three major inefficiencies associated with the rigid salary schedules employed in most school districts today.[31] First, in districts with many schools, the schedules suppress differences across schools—teachers in dozens, or perhaps hundreds, of schools have their pay set by the same salary schedule. The diverse conditions of work at different schools are not recognized, and, since most collective bargaining agreements dictate that interschool transfers must be based on seniority, more experienced teachers sometimes abandon tough schools for less challenging work environments. While greater teacher experience does not necessarily translate into higher student achievement, teachers with longer tenure can provide useful information on instructional programs (including unsuccessful innovations used in the past) and historical information on students encountering academic or personal difficulties.

Second, the single salary schedule does not allow for different pay for teachers in different fields. According to Michael Podgursky, "If you had to design a compensation system to produce teacher shortages, this would be it."[32] While the typical school district may have an adequate pool of applicants in some areas (for example, elementary or physical education teachers), many face severe shortages in the fields of special education, math, and science. In a market-based compensation system, relative pay in these and other high-demand fields would rise, but the single-salary schedule prevents such adjustment.

Finally, the single-salary schedule fails to reward superior performance or effort. Districts across the country continue to base pay on experience and educational attainment, despite a growing body of evidence suggesting that additional years of experience and extra educational credits do not necessarily pay off in greater classroom effectiveness.[33] For example, a recent RAND study analyzed National Assessment of Educational Progress scores from 44 states for the years 1990 through 1996 and concluded that "higher educational levels and increased experience...do not show significant effects on achievement."[34]

With such studies questioning the value of the single-salary schedule, several districts have begun to experiment with alternative approaches to teacher compensation, leading to fresh thinking about how to better align teachers' pay with student achievement objectives.

# MERIT PAY

Following the publication of *A Nation at Risk* in 1983, many school systems developed merit-pay programs. These were often implemented in conjunction with career-ladder systems, and in many of these plans, almost all teachers received some type of incentive regardless of performance.[35] As Jacobson found in his study of these programs, "awards were given inconspicuously to almost all teachers, so as to minimize disappointment and competitiveness."[36] None of the new systems based salary differentials exclusively on differences in performance.

Due, in part, to the opposition of teachers, these early merit-pay efforts were unsuccessful.[37] Decisions regarding merit pay were based largely on evaluations performed by the principal,[38] and teachers were uncomfortable basing differences in pay on such subjective judgments.[39] In this regard, Albert Shanker, the late president of the American Federation of Teachers, commented, "Most teachers oppose merit pay because it often has nothing to do with merit and everything to do with how well you get along with the principal."[40] Merit-pay programs also caused ill will and resentment among colleagues. Individuals competed for incentive-program monies,[41] and some teachers resented peers who helped design the programs. Other teachers resisted peer evaluations as a threat to their autonomy. From their perspective, change brought about by the actions of fellow teachers was no different than change brought about by any other external authority.[42]

But perhaps the most important obstacle to the success of merit-pay programs was simply teachers' resistance to change. Teachers worried about losing their jobs, fretted over their abilities, and feared rejection.[43] They were used to getting regular pay increases—regardless of their classroom performance—and found it frightening to consider tying raises to evaluations that, in some instances, amounted to comparisons with other teachers. As one teacher commented, "I would be utterly devastated to apply for promotion and not make it. It would cause me to consider getting out of teaching."[44] Others were reluctant to participate in career ladders and merit-pay programs because they valued their time away from school and were concerned that these programs would interfere with their already busy lives.[45] Many teachers who were to receive merit pay often took on extra responsibilities, such as acting as a mentor, composing portfolios, and providing assistance to other teachers, but did not receive extra compensation due to cutbacks in funding.[46]

# PORTFOLIOS

To overcome teachers' concerns about basing merit pay on principal or peer evaluations, some school systems created compensation plans that based incentives on alternative measures of performance. For example, in Douglas County, Colorado, district administrators encouraged teachers to submit portfolios—including, among other things, a resumé; a philosophy of education statement; commentaries on assessment, instruction, content, pedagogy, and other topics; a recent district evaluation or professional growth plan; and a self-evaluation. Those teachers deemed "outstanding" were awarded a $1,000 bonus.[47] During the program's inaugural year, a full 90 percent of the teachers who participated earned bonuses.[48]

Douglas County still uses the portfolio program today, as both teachers and administrators are pleased with the results. Still, there are a number of potential problems with this approach—especially the program's strong reliance on subjective and self-evaluative criteria. Equally troubling is the program's provision that allows evaluators to consider information not included in the portfolio. As proponents of the program explained, "while recognizing the risk of allowing administrators to go beyond the portfolio in assigning their ratings, the committee believed that it provided an important safeguard for the program, particularly in the case of a teacher whose portfolio was exemplary, but whose teaching or professional conduct was not."[49] This leads one to ask that if the administrators already know who the outstanding teachers are, why bother with a portfolio program?

# COMPETENCY- AND SKILL-BASED PAY

As an alternative to merit-pay and portfolio programs, a number of scholars have proposed competency-based or skill-based pay plans.[50] Such programs would reward teachers for developing three types of skills: depth skills (content knowledge or pedagogical skills); breadth skills (nonteaching responsibilities, such as parent outreach, professional development, and guidance counseling);

11

and management skills (skills relevant to the operation of site-based managed schools).[51]

Skill-based plans, proponents argue, base pay more directly on a teacher's knowledge than do compensation systems based on the traditional single-salary schedule. They limit competition within the faculty by rewarding teachers on the basis of their mastery of certain skills, rather than on the basis of comparisons with their colleagues.

Allen Odden has suggested that teachers should be compensated according to their progress in completing specific professional development benchmarks, such as passing the Praxis exams from the Educational Testing Service[52] and achieving state board certification.[53] Others have proposed variations of this approach, but increasingly, much of the discussion of skill-based pay centers around the work of the National Board for Professional Teaching Standards (NBPTS).

# National Board for Professional Teaching Standards

Created in 1987, the National Board for Professional Teaching Standards is a nonprofit educational organization devoted to the development of a comprehensive teacher evaluation system as part of a broad initiative to raise standards for the teaching profession by recognizing exemplary practice. Teachers who are candidates for the national accreditation offered by the National Board are scored on 10 performance assessments over the course of a year.[54] Six of the assessments are based on a teacher's portfolio, which includes items such as videotapes of classroom performance, comments and analyses of students' work, and commentaries on the teacher's work outside of the classroom. Although some states and districts give teachers paid leave to compile these portfolios (for example, Arkansas, Georgia, and Phoenix, Arizona), most often they must complete this work on their own time.[55] The remaining four assessments are computer-based tests that simulate various classroom practices and ask teachers to design a curriculum and assess student learning, among other things.[56]

The National Board's certification process has received a great deal of support from educators and policy makers as a promising step toward increasing teacher quality. As of June 2001, 44 states offered financial support to teachers who earn board certification, including reimbursement of the $2,000 application fee. Some states offer $10,000 yearly bonuses for the life of the certificate and salary increases of 12 percent or more for teachers who obtain this certification.[57] Thus far, the federal government has appropriated $90.8 million for NBPTS—more than half (55 percent) of the cost of developing the program.[58] The National Board's goal is to certify 105,000 teachers by 2006, or about one board-certified teacher for every school in the nation.[59] As of January 2001, a total of 9,531 teachers had been certified.

The National Board's certification process offers excellent opportunities for teachers to reflect on their teaching philosophies and practices, collaborate with colleagues on curricula and instructional practices, and analyze their strengths and weaknesses within the classroom. Board certification should be acknowledged as an honor and achievement, as it indicates that the teacher was able to meet or exceed standards set by fellow educators (the majority of the 63-member board of directors are classroom teachers). Further, unlike merit-pay plans, skill-based compensation plans based on National Board certification are embraced by teachers and receive strong support from the two national teachers' unions, the National Education Association and the American Federation of Teachers.

But some critics note that problems remain, both with the NBPTS evaluation method and its guiding philosophy. Anthony Milanowski and his coauthors have raised several key questions:

- Is the limited number of observations involved in these assessments a sufficient basis for making a reliable decision about a teacher's knowledge and skill?

- Since portfolios may represent best rather than typical performance, will certified teachers actually practice at the level at which they were assessed?

- Is teacher performance as assessed in a single context—typically via observations, videos, or portfolio artifacts drawn from one class or one school—representative of likely performance in another class or another school? For example, might a teacher who passes these assessments in a culturally homogenous upper-middle-class school fail them within the context of a culturally diverse, lower-socioeconomic school?[60]

Critics also note that the National Board's approach to assessing the portfolios of certification candidates is also problematic. For example, Klein has observed that "raters who graded a response of medium quality gave a lower score when it was presented with high-quality responses and a higher score when the other responses were of poor quality."[61] But even if such questions about NBPTS scoring were resolved, districts that base teacher compensation on NBPTS certification may be vulnerable to legal action from teachers who are denied pay raises because of poor performance on the tests.[62] Were a minority candidate to take the assessment, fail to be certified, and be denied a pay increase, a prima facie case of discrimination under Title VII of the Civil Rights Act may exist, providing grounds for legal action. Certainly, in portfolios (and their accompanying videos), the race of the candidate is typically revealed to the scorer. Defending the NBPTS assessment in court might be difficult, too, because of the scant evidence linking certification to classroom effectiveness.

In an effort to determine whether this linkage exists, the University of North Carolina published a study in September 2000. It reached a promising conclusion from a sampling of 65 teachers: those teachers certified by the National Board demonstrated the attributes of expert teaching to a greater degree than teachers not certified by the Board. However, several significant criticisms of the research methodology used make this one study of the National Board's system less than convincing evidence of the program's impact on classroom effectiveness.[63]

There is a critical need for more and better research evaluating the relationship between National Board certification and classroom performance. To defuse legal attacks, reward systems must be validated, and direct relationships between compensation and teacher effectiveness must be established so that school systems avoid any claim of discrimination. As Robert Heneman and Gerald Ledford point out, "Educational organizations cannot escape the possibility of legal liability if their competency systems discriminate against protected groups and appropriate evidence of validity is unavailable. It should be noted that basing competency pay on the available national certification standards is no guarantee of legal protection."[64] Unfortunately, this problem is likely to go unresolved, at least for the near future, since the only plan for a more rigorous evaluation of NBPTS certification will not produce results for several more years.

Meanwhile, for policy makers, the lack of solid evidence linking National Board evaluation standards with increased student performance should raise questions about their value in teacher compensation systems. NBPTS-based compensation plans reward teachers for something done *outside* the classroom and for work not directly tied to student achievement. Incentives are based on

*"In the private sector, there is a substantial body of evidence linking pay-for-performance compensation strategies to higher levels of productivity."*

subjective measures developed by an abstract peer group on performance measures that have little or nothing to do with actual classroom performance. Potentially, students of a board-certified teacher could show dramatic declines in student achievement, yet the teacher could still receive incentive money for completing the board-certification process. Conversely, a teacher with a record of exemplary classroom performance who increased student achievement dramatically, developed outreach programs for disadvantaged children, and mentored new teachers, would not receive incentive pay if she did not complete board certification. Finally, many NBPTS-based compensation plans reward teachers with a bonus for the 10-year life of the certificate. Even if subsequent research reveals that board certification is associated with higher student achievement in the short run, the relationship may well weaken over the long run. A teacher who was highly effective 10 years ago may be burned out today.

14

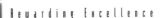

In these and other respects, compensation systems based primarily on NBPTS or similar standards are questionable and perhaps fundamentally flawed—in much the same way as the single-salary schedule. Both approaches measure *inputs* to teaching, not *outcomes*—particularly, student achievement. NBPTS proponents assume that any teacher who earns national certification will contribute to students' learning, but research does not yet support this assumption. In the absence of studies linking national assessments and student achievement, using these assessments as proxies for teacher effectiveness is not currently justified. A better alternative to assessing teacher quality would be to evaluate teacher outcomes directly.

# ASSESSING OUTCOMES

Despite a history of failed experiments with merit pay, there are strong theoretical reasons for believing that well-structured compensation systems that reward teachers for their performance will elicit higher levels of effort and productivity.[65] Indeed, in the private sector, there is a substantial body of evidence linking pay-for-performance compensation strategies to higher levels of productivity,[66] and, in Dallas, Charles Clotfelter and Helen Ladd found a statistically significant positive impact on achievement that they attributed to the district's accountability and reward system.[67]

A number of states and school districts have implemented compensation systems that pay teachers in part based on student-achievement indicators, such as standardized test scores, graduation rates, dropout percentages, attendance statistics, and promotion figures. The data are most often aggregated to the school or even district level for the purpose of making compensation decisions at the school level. School-wide rewards are used to avoid some of the inherent problems with merit-pay programs, such as competition among teachers. Also, there is a growing recognition that gains in student achievement are not solely the result of an individual teacher but a reflection of the overall learning environment.[68] Many researchers believe that school-level incentives encourage collaboration between teachers and improve student achievement outcomes.[69]

In many accountability programs that tie school and teacher incentives to student outcomes, teachers can earn bonuses in amounts ranging from a few hundred dollars to a few thousand dollars. For example, in 1995, the first year that rewards were given as part of the Kentucky Instructional Results Information System (KIRIS), $25.5 million was allocated to schools, providing incentives for some 14,100 teachers and administrators. Depending on the school's allocation of those funds, teacher bonuses ranged from $1,301 to $2,602.[70] As part of Dallas's accountability program, principals and teachers of schools showing the most progress earn $1,000 and nonprofessional staff earns $500. Other teachers and principals who perform better than expected earn $450 bonuses, and the nonprofessional personnel earn $225.[71]

As discussed earlier in this report (see "Objective Evaluations," page 4), many educators resist Dallas-like accountability plans that use student-achievement indicators. A recent study conducted by *Phi Delta Kappan* indicated that only 3 percent of teachers felt that students' standardized test scores should be a "very important" factor in determining teachers' salaries. These critics have legitimate concerns that badly designed accountability plans can lead to narrowing of the curriculum, cheating, and a bias against schools with disproportionate numbers of disadvantaged students.

But more sophisticated accountability systems can be designed to more accurately measure the value added by schools exclusive of nonschool-related influences. Additionally, efforts to artificially boost student scores—and, therefore, teacher compensation—can be determined by using multiple standardized exams and by imposing severe sanctions on schools and teachers who breach test security.[72]

This is not to say that today's best accountability programs are perfect. Even the most sophisticated compensation systems are too complex for most teachers and administrators to understand. And if educators don't understand the factors measured in an accountability system, the system won't work as it should. For example, some administrators in Dallas find it difficult to explain how the system works to rank-and-file teachers, which undermines morale and confidence in the program.[73]

Clearly, value-added assessments and accountability programs that tie teacher pay to student performance are in the early stages of development and require constant reevaluation and work. A number of educators, for example, have questioned whether Kentucky's accountability system encourages low-achieving students to drop out of school, thus inflating school-level scores. As one assessment coordinator in Kentucky stated, "I'm concerned because we have fewer students after grade nine, and it looks like it's to a school's advantage to get a kid to drop out rather than to keep him in the rolls and have poor test scores at grade 12."[74] Interestingly, Kentucky has attempted to combat such problems with its accountability system by using student portfolios instead of standardized test scores as indicators of student achievement. Although this method has promise, there remain serious concerns regarding reliability of this approach (see, for example, the sidebar on Vermont's experiment with student portfolios). A number of scholars have suggested that "hybrid" assessments be developed to combine the strengths of standardized test scores with the strengths of performance-based indicators.[75]

Despite the need for such fine-tuning, accountability systems with teacher-pay provisions appear to hold the most promise for improving learning. As Meyer concludes, "If policy makers are serious about holding schools and districts accountable for their contributions to growth in student achievement, it is crucial to quantify that contribution in a valid and accurate manner using student outcome measures that accurately reflect educational goals."[76] And if experimental pay-for-performance programs are to be brought to scale, it will be critical that school districts evaluate them. In the absence of indisputable evidence of the effectiveness of such programs, union opposition will not be easily overcome.[77]

# The Vermont Experiment:
# Can Student Portfolios Be Used as Evidence of Achievement?

To address some limitations of measuring student achievement using standardized test scores, Vermont in 1988 implemented an accountability program using portfolios as the primary measure of student performance. However, outside researchers found a number of problems with this evaluation method. Specifically, reliability from rater to rater was very low, meaning that two scorers evaluating the same student's work rated the portfolios very differently.[78] Furthermore, relationships between ratings on portfolios and ratings on standardized tests were very weak or nonexistent. One particular study indicated that two-thirds of the students rated competent based on their writing portfolio were found less than competent based on their standardized test scores.[79] The discrepancy in scores may have been due in part to the collaborative nature of portfolios, where teachers and peers contribute to the student's work, thereby making it difficult to assess the individual student's achievement level. By 1996, the Vermont State School Board mandated standardized testing to supplement the portfolio system. As one state educator commented, "Portfolios provide rich information about some very specific student skills and knowledge, but we were concerned about their use for accountability."[80]

# Conclusions and Recommendations

T eacher evaluation and compensation remain controversial issues, in part because the best approaches are not entirely clear. At the same time, recent studies suggest that the single-salary schedule is not conducive to higher student achievement and may even present significant barriers to reducing the gap between privileged and disadvantaged children. Raising teacher salaries across the board—another popular move—is equally ineffective, according to most studies.[82]

For this reason alone, there is a strong movement toward implementing pay-for-performance compensation systems that allow poor teachers to be weeded out and excellent teachers to be rewarded. Many experiments in evaluation and compensation today tinker with the current single-salary structure while accepting its premise—that years of experience and training are the measures of a good teacher. But to truly affect student performance, reformers and administrators must be willing to reject that premise and embrace the idea that the ultimate measure of a teacher is whether his or her students are learning. The performance that must be assessed and rewarded is *actual classroom performance*, rather than performance on exams, certifications, or other input factors that have not been demonstrated to be linked with productivity in the classroom.

The first step in making these major changes in compensation is to obtain the tools necessary to accurately assess teacher performance. The value-added assessment system provides promise in revamping teacher evaluation and, subsequently, teacher compensation. These assessments, coupled with 360-degree evaluations, should provide a bounty of invaluable information—information about a teacher's effectiveness in the classroom, information about student learning, and information that could be used to more closely align compensation with performance.

# Key Findings

The quality of teachers has emerged as an issue of paramount importance to improving student achievement.

Subjective methods of evaluating teachers—that is, observations by principals, student and parent appraisals, and peer review—do not provide a direct, concrete measure of whether the teacher is contributing to a child's learning and should be used in conjunction with objective assessments.

Value-added assessments, coupled with 360-degree assessments, are likely to be more effective at measuring teacher quality than the traditional observation by the principal.

The fundamental law of the single-salary schedule is that it measures teacher inputs, not student learning outcomes.

Research demonstrates that across-the-board pay increases and higher starting salaries for new teachers do not positively affect student achievement.

Using national teacher certification as a proxy for teacher effectiveness is not yet justified.

Pay-for-performance plans that reward teachers at the school level can avoid some problems of merit-pay programs.

Accountability systems with payment provisions for teachers appear to hold the most promise for improving learning.

The teachers' unions argue that pay-for-performance has been tried—unsuccessfully—in merit-pay plans. But to avoid the problems of those programs—including competition among teachers—rewards could be given to teams or to entire schools to encourage collaboration and teamwork. Career ladders where teachers move in steps from novice to professional teacher status also could be implemented to give teachers upward mobility—something obviously lacking in the profession, but perhaps key to attracting prospective teachers.

# AT THE STATE LEVEL

Those interested in shaping their state's legislative agenda need to convey to legislators that the century-old methods of teacher evaluation and compensation are outdated and need to be replaced with a system more directly linked to objective measures of student achievement. To date, the biggest opponents to such change have been the teachers' unions. As the Education Commission of the States pointed out in a recent report, "Many of the newer ideas and trends, such as recruitment incentives, market-driven salaries, pay and promotion based on demonstrated skill and performance, and alternative routes into the teaching profession, cannot be readily accommodated by the present union contracts and collective-bargaining practices."[82] Indeed, teachers' unions are so adamantly opposed to incentive-pay plans that they often would rather strike than accept such proposals, which is what nearly happened in Los Angeles in April 2000.[83]

Given the history of failed merit-pay efforts, it is understandable why teachers' unions resist such compensation strategies. However, the tools used to evaluate teacher performance have changed dramatically since merit-pay programs were introduced, and more accurate measures of teacher performance are now available. Further, there are a number of ways to

*"The quality of teachers has emerged as an issue of paramount importance in improving student achievement."*

allocate funds for performance, such as giving team-based or school-based awards, which would minimize rivalry among teachers and remove any incentive for individual teachers to allow students to cheat on tests in order to boost their apparent performance.

Lawmakers also must recognize that it will take substantial resources to develop, implement, and maintain effective accountability and performance evaluation systems. The personnel effort for these more complex evaluation systems is great; a team of qualified researchers (consultants) must develop and implement the programs, and analysts are needed to decipher results and fine-tune the system. The accountability program used in Dallas, for example, is the product of three decades of continuous conceptualization, redefinitions, and retooling. At one point, the research and development unit in the Dallas school system employed 40 Ph.D. specialists in evaluation.[84]

Accountability programs require substantial funding to pay salaries for research and development personnel and to buy data-analysis equipment, norm-referenced tests, and other evaluative tools. Money also must be appropriated for bonuses to reward those schools and teachers meeting targeted student-achievement goals.

The accountability movement is more than a decade old, and the past holds many lessons for lawmakers. Fortunately, a number of states and districts have already developed value-added accountability programs, and a great deal of research has been conducted on best practices within this arena. The Dallas Independent School System, for example, has an extensive Web page devoted to its accountability program, and its research and development team is continuously presenting papers and discussions. William Sanders, the developer of the Tennessee Value-Added Assessment System, has also consulted on many value-added assessment projects. Such exchanges of ideas and knowledge will ultimately lead to the most effective assessment system.

# AT THE DISTRICT LEVEL

At the district level, school officials must commit to evaluating all teachers, not just nontenured educators. Because teacher effectiveness is crucial to student achievement, it is imperative that teachers understand their strengths and weaknesses so they can continually improve. Furthermore, principals need to identify weak teachers in order to provide necessary assistance. Superintendents and school board members, meanwhile, need this evaluation information to help make hiring, firing, and compensation decisions. (See Appendix C for a number of critical questions that school board members should ask).

Schools should also aim to evaluate teachers in the most complete fashion possible, using both subjective and objective data. And these evaluations must be based on classroom performance—how well the teacher "gives knowledge" to

*"School boards also should move ... toward pay-for-performance plans that provide incentives for strong teacher performance."*

her students and prepares them for the world ahead. To this end, local officials should explore using value-added assessments in conjunction with 360-degree assessments. Understanding exactly how students perform under the direction and guidance of a particular teacher is fundamental to increasing student achievement. Further, 360-degree evaluations provide feedback from parents, students, teachers, and other colleagues that foster ongoing dialogue and continual improvement.

School boards also should move away from the traditional single-salary schedule toward pay-for-performance plans that provide incentives for strong teacher performance. Research has shown that across-the board pay increases do not have a positive impact on student achievement. It may be more effective to use these funds to pay signing bonuses to talented teacher candidates, a plan recently adopted by the state of Massachusetts. Or districts might give bonuses to schools that meet predetermined goals, which many states do in conjunction with newly implemented accountability programs.

Though most accountability programs have been built at the state level, districts such as the Dallas Independent School System have undertaken the task as well. As with states, districts will find that securing the resources for developing and implementing such a program is a key obstacle. Funds can come from a variety of sources, including the federal government and business communities. The Dallas business community, for example, offset some of the costs of that district's accountability program, contributing half of the $2.5 million given to teachers as performance awards.[86]

Districts should also conduct a budget review with an eye to trimming programs that aren't substantially linked to improving student learning. Some critics assert that school districts often allocate funds toward efforts that essentially do not affect learning.[87] By evaluating the purpose and efficacy of programs, personnel, and policies that are not directly tied to raising student achievement, school districts may find resources they need while not jeopardizing other vital school programs.

# Appendix A
## Approaches to Teacher Evaluation

| Evaluation Method | Criteria Considered | Objective/ Subjective | Strengths | Weaknesses | Linked to Student Achievement |
|---|---|---|---|---|---|
| Observations by principals | Teacher's instructional style; teacher-student interactions; classroom environment | Subjective | Easy to admnister. Acceptable to teachers. | Performance of teacher is based on only one or two observations. Evaluations by principals are often inflated. | No |
| Student evaluations | Teacher-student interactions; students' ability to learn from teacher | Subjective | Performance is based on large data sample (many interactions with teacher throughout school year). Shown to have greatest reliability. | May encourage grade inflation (teacher gives good grades to recieve good evalutions). Students are not unbiased observers. | No |
| Parent evaluations | How teacher interacts with child and family; responds to student's needs; assigns challenging homework; inspires student to learn | Subjective | Performance is based on large data sample (many interactions with teacher throughout school year). Teachers value parent feedback. | May encourage grade inflation (teacher gives good grades to receive good evalutions). Parents are not unbiased observers. | No |

| Evaluation Method | Criteria Considered | Objective/ Subjective | Strengths | Weaknesses | Linked to Student Achievement |
|---|---|---|---|---|---|
| Peer evaluations | How teacher interacts with students; classroom discipline; effectiveness of lessons; knowledge of subject matter | Subjective | Performance is based on large data sample. Peers can give contstructive feedback and offer suggestions for improve-ment. | Lack of direct knowledge of teacher's performance.* Conflict of interest—teachers may collaborate to give each other good evaluations. | No |
| Self-evaluations | Effectiveness of lesson plans; discipline strategies; interactions with students and parents. | Subjective | Opportunity for self-reflection and analysis of his/her strengths and weaknesses with regard to subject matter knowledge and pedagogy. | Teachers may be resistant to peer evaluations. Teacher may be reluctant to admit to weaknesses. Not an unbiased observer. | No |
| Value-added assessments | Standardized test scores using pre- and post-test outcomes | Objective | Allows evaluators to assess contribution teacher made to student performance during the academic year. It is an unbiased measure. | Teachers are resistant to this type of evaluation. May provoke undesirable behavior such as cheating or teaching to the test. | Yes |

*Peer evaluations should be completed only by individuals with direct knowledge of the teacher's performance, such as a reading teacher who works in the teacher's classroom, or another teacher in the same discipline who has collaborated with the teacher being evaluated.

# Appendix B
## Approaches to Teacher Compensation

| Compensation Plan | Criteria Considered | Input or Outcome | Objective/Subjective | Strengths | Weaknesses | Linked to Student Achievement |
|---|---|---|---|---|---|---|
| Single-salary schedule | Years of experience; educational credits | Input | Objective | Easy to administer. Popular with teachers. Seen as fair and equitable by teachers. | No accountability. Does not distinguish between high- and low-quality teachers. | No |
| Merit-pay and career ladder programs | Evaluation of teacher by principal | Outcome | Subjective | Pays for performance and attempts to distinguish between high- and low-quality teachers. | Unpopular with teachers. Seen as unfair and based on teacher-principal relationship. Creates competition among teachers. Possible lack of funding. | No |
| Merit-pay and career ladder programs | Additional teacher responsibility | Input | Objective | Gives teachers a sense of empowerment and expanded role. Facilitates mentorships. Distinguishes between high- and low-quality teachers. | Creates competition among teachers. Possible lack of funding for continued programs. May not provide opportunities for all qualified teachers. | No |

27

| Compensation Plan | Criteria Considered | Input or Outcome | Objective/ Subjective | Strengths | Weaknesses | Linked to Student Achievement |
|---|---|---|---|---|---|---|
| Skill-based pay | Interstate New Teacher Assessment & Support Consortium (INTASC) and National Board for Professional Teaching Standards assessments | Input | Both subjective and objective | Popular with teacher organizations. No competition among teachers. Encourages teachers to acquire skills that may be useful in classroom performance. | Assessment not tied to classroom performance. May present legal problems and adverse impact cases. Assesses best performance rather than typical performance. | No |
| Skill-based pay | Praxis exams | Input | Objective | No competition among teachers. Encourages teachers to acquire skills that may be useful in classroom performance. | Assessment not tied to classroom performance. Exam may not be rigorous enough to distinguish high- and low-quality teachers. | No |
| Student performance | Student standardized test scores; value-added | Outcome | Objective | Allows evaluators to assess contributions teachers made to student performance during the academic year. Helps identify high- and low-quality teachers. | Very unpopular with teachers. May provoke undesirable behavior such as teaching to the test and cheating. Difficult and costly to administer. Does not capture higher-order skills. | Yes |
| Student performance | Student portfolios | Outcome | Subjective | Allows evaluation of higher-order skills and provides actual classroom artifacts. Assesses skills throughout the year instead of one point in time. | Problems with reliability and validity of assessment. Does not reflect individual student performance. Difficult to use in comparing students/schools. | Yes |
| Other | Teacher portfolios | Input | Subjective | Allows a variety of materials to be evaluated and assesses performance for entire year, not just one point in time. | No accountability. Problems with reliability and validity of assessment. Does not reflect individual performance. | No |

# Appendix C
## Questions about Compensation and Evaluation

When meeting with superintendents and other central office staff, school board members should raise the topic of teacher evaluation and compensation. One place to start would be to request that the superintendent discuss the current compensation and evaluation system with the school board and talk about developing a process for considering possible alternatives. The following questions might be helpful to gauging the quality of your district's initiatives in this area:

- Does your school district evaluate teachers? How was that system developed? Was the union involved? If so, how?

- What staff resources are committed to ensuring thorough review of teachers?

- What is the teachers' union position on pay-for-performance plans?

- What programs and budget expenditures are not directly related to improving student achievement?

- What data-analysis equipment is available to the district?

- Are teachers being encouraged to pursue certification by the National Board for Professional Teaching Standards?

- Is your teacher evaluation system aligned with the student achievement goals of the district?

- Does your school district focus on teacher performance, student achievement, or other mechanisms?

- Has your school district considered using a value-added system to evaluate teacher effectiveness?

- On a school-by-school basis, what nonteacher factors are present that could influence the effectiveness of teachers to raise student achievement?

# Endnotes

[1] Kelly, C. (1997).

[2] Webster, W. (1997).

[3] National Commission on Excellence in Education, (1983) A Nation at Risk.

[4] Stronge, J. (1997).

[5] Evertson, C., & Holley, F. (1981).

[6] Stronge, J. (1997).

[7] In one study, Ostrander (1995) found that "principals consistently rated the teachers higher than any of the other respondents on all subcategories except homework, where the teacher self-assessments were higher. The students gave the teachers the lowest rating in all areas; the parents' rating showed a higher correlation with student ratings than with teacher or principal ratings" (Stronge & Ostrander, 1997:142).

[8] Stronge, J., & Ostrander, L. (1997).

[9] Larson, R. (1984).

[10] Ebmeier, H., Jenkins, R., & Crawford, G. (1991).

[11] Aleamoni, L. (1981).

[12] Epstein (1985) as cited in Stronge and Ostrander (1997).

[13] Peterson, K. (1988).

[14] Epstein (1985:4) as cited in Stronge and Ostrander (1997).

[15] Stronge, J., & Ostrander, L. (1997).

[16] Education Commission of the States (2000:1).

[17] Webster, W. (1997).

[18] Goodnough, A. (1999); Koretz, D. (1996).

[19] Meyers, R. (1996).

[20] A recent study of North Carolina's accountability system by Kane and Staiger (2001) found that most of the variation in one-year gains of students taught by different teachers and the average gains of students in different schools stems from measurement error and single-year occurrences in schools rather than from persistent differences in programs or teacher effectiveness. To circumvent this problem, these authors advocate using weighted averages of test score gains over several years and offer a clever strategy for determining the appropriate weights.

[21] Bembry, K., Bearden, D., & Mendro, R. (1997).

[22] Bembry et al. (1997).

[23] Webster, W. (1997).

[24] Sanders, W., & Horn, S. (1998).

[25] A recent study of South Carolina's accountability system—which, like Sanders' approach, focuses on gain scores calculated solely from student test scores—suggests that his assertion may not hold up under empirical examination (Clotfelter & Ladd, 1997). The authors of the study conclude that

31

evaluation models that adjust student test scores for previous performance, but not for socioeconomic status, will fall short, because socioeconomic status affects not only the level of achievement but also its rate of growth. Another study, by Hanushek, Kain, and Rivkin (2001), points out that, even after controlling for student background characteristics, students enrolled in schools with high mobility rates tend to achieve at a slow rate.

[26] Sanders, W., & Horn, S. (1998).

[27] Stronge, J. (1997:4).

[28] Stronge, J. (1997).

[29] Another important use for the information derived from teacher evaluation systems—identifying teachers in need of professional development—will be addressed in the third and final report in this series.

[30] Kelley, C., & Odden, A. (1995).

[31] Thanks to Michael Podgursky for identifying these inefficiencies in his review comments.

[32] Quoted from Michael Podgursky's review comments (p. 2).

[33] Hanushek, E. (1986, 1996).

[34] Grissmer, D., Flanagan, A., Kawata, J., & Williamson, S. (2000:99).

[35] Brandt, R. (1990).

[36] Jacobson (1989) as cited in Brandt (1990).

[37] Firestone, W. (1991).

[38] Firestone, W. (1991); Arthur, G., & Milton, S. (1991).

[39] Odden, A. (n.d.).

[40] Shanker, A. (1995).

[41] Kelley, C., & Odden, A. (1995).

[42] Fullan, M., & Stieglbauer, S. (1991:127).

[43] Mohrman, S., & Lawler, E. (1996).

[44] Brandt, R. (1990).

[45] Brandt, R. (1990).

[46] Arthur, G., & Milton, S. (1991).

[47] Wolf, K., Lichtenstein, G., Bartlett, E., & Hartman, D. (1996).

[48] Wolf, K. et al. (1996).

[49] Wolf, K. et al. (1996:284).

[5] Kelley, C. (1997); Odden, A. (2000).

[51] Kelley, C., & Odden, A. (1995).

[52] See Sullivan, C. (2001), in the first report in NSBA's series on teacher effectiveness for a discussion of the Praxis tests.

[53] Odden, A. (2000).

[54] Jaeger, R. (1998); National Education Association (1999).

[55] National Education Association (1999).

[56] Jaeger, R. (1998); National Board for Professional Teaching Standards (2001).

[57] National Board for Professional Teaching Standards (2001).

[58] National Board for Professional Teaching Standards (2001).

[59] Darling-Hammond, L. (2000).

[60] Milanowski, A., Odden, A., & Youngs, P. (1998:95).

[61] Klein, S. (1998) as cited in Milanowski et al. (1998:95-96).

[62] As Milanowski, Odden, and Youngs (1998:89) found, "While the proportions of women and men

passing the NBPTS assessments has not typically differed, African-American candidates were certified in lower proportions than non-Hispanic whites and the difference is great enough to conclude, using the 80 percent rule, that the NBPTS assessments have an adverse impact on African-Americans."

[63] In a study conducted by the University of North Carolina at Greensboro (Bond, Smith, Baker & Hattie, 2000), researchers concluded that students taught by NBPTS-certified teachers fared better than their peers. Specifically, they found that students taught by Board-certified teachers "differ in profound and important ways from those taught by less proficient teachers. These students appear to exhibit an understanding of the concepts targeted in instruction that is more integrated, more coherent, and at a higher level of abstraction than understandings achieved by other students." While these findings are intriguing, they are not the product of a rigorous research design model. Most critically, the researchers failed to pre-test students, so that there was no means of determining whether their advanced skills were acquired while in class with their NBPTS teacher or before. Podgursky (2001) finds fault with the study on several other grounds, including its "circular" approach to assessing teacher expertise. In his rebuttal, Bond (2001) takes issue with Podgursky's critique, but does not provide a serious defense of the study's principal weakness—its failure to control for the pre-assessment ability of its subjects. Rather, he notes simply that "it was duly noted in the study that the unavailability of appropriate covariates for these measures implies that differences in student achievement could not be unambiguously attributable to teachers" (Bond, 2001:3).

[64] Heneman, R., & Ledford, G. (1998:111).

[65] Pencavel, J. (1977); Brown (1990).

[66] Mitchell D., Lewin, D., & Lawler, E. (1990); Weitzman, M., & Kruse, D. (1990). For a review of performance-based pay, see Blinder, A. (1990).

[67] Clotfelter, C., & Ladd, H. (1997).

[68] Clotfelter, C., & Ladd, H. (1997).

[69] Kelley, C., & Odden, A. (1995).

[70] Elmore, R., Abelman, C., & Fuhrman, S. (1997).

[71] Clotfelter, C., & Ladd, H. (1997).

[72] Further, teaching to the test may not be undesirable, because as Clotfelter and Ladd (1997) point out: "If the test reflects a well-designed curriculum, then teaching to the test may be exactly what the state or district intends."

[73] Clotfelter, C., and Ladd, H. (1997); Darling-Hammond, L. (1997). [

[74] Elmore et al. (1997:80).

[75] Meyer, R. (1997).

[76] Meyer, R. (1997:144).

[77] Hatrey, H., Geiner, J., and Ashford, B. (1994) surveyed 18 districts with teacher incentive plans and found that very few had attempted any systematic evaluation of their effects on student achievement.

[81] Ballou, D., & Podgursky, M. (1997); Grissmer et al. (2000).

[82] Education Commission of the States (2000).

[83] American Federation of Teachers (2000).

[84] Cunningham, L. (1997).

[85] Clotfelter, C., & Ladd, H. (1997).

[86] Hanushek, E. (1996).

[78] Viadero, D. (1993).

[79] Gearhart, M., & Herman, J. (1995).

[80] Manzo, K. (1996).

# References

Aleamoni, L. (1981). Student ratings of instruction. In J. Millman (Ed.), *Handbook of teacher evaluation.* Beverly Hills, CA: Sage Publications.

American Federation of Teachers. (2000). *AFT on the Issues: Merit pay.* [On-line]. Available: http://www.aft.org/issues/Meritpay/turmoil.html.

Arthur, G., & Milton, S. (1991). The Florida teacher incentive program: A policy analysis. *Educational Policy, 5* (3), 266-278.

Ballou, D., & Podgursky, M. (1997). *Teacher pay and teacher quality.* Kalamazoo, MI: W.E. Upjohn Institute for Employment Research.

Bembry, K., Bearden, D., & Mendro, R. (1997, March). *Using student achievement in teacher appraisal.* Paper presented at the annual meeting of the American Educational Research Association, Chicago, IL.

Blinder, A. (1990). *Paying for productivity: A look at the evidence.* Washington, DC: The Brookings Institution.

Bond, L. (2001) On "defrocking the National Board": A reply to Podgursky. Greensboro, NC: Department of Educational Research Methodology & Center for Educational Research and Evaluation, University of North Carolina at Greensboro.

Bond, L., Smith, T., Baker, W., & Hattie, J. (2000). *The certification system of the National Board for Professional Teaching Standards: A construct and consequential validity study.* Greensboro, NC: Department of Educational Research Methodology & Center for Educational Research and Evaluation, University of North Carolina at Greensboro.

Brandt, R. (1990). *Incentive pay and career ladders for today's teachers.* Albany, NY: State University of New York.

Brown, Charles (1990). "Firms Choice of Method of Pay." *Industrial and Labor Relations Review*, 43.

Clotfelter, C., & Ladd, H. (1997). Recognizing and rewarding success in public schools. In H. Ladd (Ed.), *Holding schools accountable* (pp. 23-63). Washington, D.C.: Brookings Institution Press.

35

Cunningham, L. (1997). In the beginning. In J. Millman (Ed.), *Grading teachers, grading schools* (pp. 75-80). Thousand Oaks, CA: Corwin Press.

Darling-Hammond, L. (1997). Toward what end? The evaluation of student learning for the improvement of teaching. In J. Millman (Ed.), *Grading teachers, grading schools* (pp. 248-263). Thousand Oaks, CA: Corwin Press.

Darling-Hammond, L. (2000). *Two paths to quality teaching. Implications for policymakers.* Denver, CO: Education Commission of the States.

Ebmeier, H., Jenkins, R., & Crawford, G. (199 1). The predicitive validity of student evaluations in the identification of meritorious teachers. *Journal of Personnel Evaluation in Education, 4*, 341-347.

Education Commission of the States. (2000). *In pursuit of quality teaching. Five key strategies for policymakers.* Denver, CO: Author.

Elmore, R., Abelman, C., & Fuhrman, S. (1997). The new accountability in state education reform: From process to performance. In H. Ladd (Ed.), *Holding schools accountable* (pp. 65-98). Washington, D.C.: Brookings Institution Press.

Evertson, C., & Holley, F. (1981). Classroom observation. In J. Millman (Ed.), *Handbook of teacher evaluation* (pp. 73-109). Beverly Hills, CA: Sage Publications.

Firestone, W. (1991). Merit pay and job enlargement as reforms: Incentives, implementation, and teacher response. *Educational Evaluation and Policy Analysis, 13* (3), 269-288.

Fullan, M., & Stieglbauer, S. (1991). *The new meaning of educational change.* New York: Teachers College Press.

Gearhart, M., & Herman, J. (1995, Winter). *Portfolio assessment: Whose work is it? Issues in the use of classroom assignments for accountability.* Los Angeles, CA: UCLA's Center for the Study of Evaluation & The National Center for Research on Evaluation, Standards, and Student Testing.

Goodnough, A. (1999, December 8). Teachers are said to aid in cheating. *The New York Times*, pp. A I, A24.

Grissmer, D., Flanagan, A., Kawata, J., & Williamson, S. (2000). *Improving student achievement—What state NAEP test scores tell us.* Santa Monica, CA: RAND.

Hanushek, E. (1986). The economics of schooling: Production and efficiency in public schools. *Journal of Economic Literature, 24* (3), 1141-1177.

Hanushek, E. (1996). Outcomes, costs and incentives in schools. In E. A. Hanushek & D. W. Jorgenson (Eds.), *Improving America's schools: The role of incentives* (pp. 29-52). Washington, D.C.: National Academy Press.

Hanushek, E., Kain, J., & Rivkin, S. (2001). Disruption versus Tiebout improvement: The costs and benefits of switching schools. Paper presented at the Summer 2001 National Bureau of Economic Research Workshop, Cambridge, MA.

Hatrey, H., Greiner, J., & Ashford, B. (1994). Issues and case studies in teacher incentive plans. Wash., D.C.: Urban Institute Press.

Heneman, R. & Ledford, G. (1998). *Competency pay for professionals and managers in business: A review and implications for teachers.* Journal of Personnel Evaluation in Education, 12 (2) 103- 21.

Jaeger, R. (1998). Evaluating the psychometric qualities of the National Board for Professional Teaching Standards assessments: A methodological accounting. *Journal of Personnel Evaluation in Education, 12* (2), 189-210.

Kane, T., and Staiger, D. (2001). Improving school accountability measures. Working paper 8156. Cambridge, Ma: National Bureau of Economic Research. Available online at http://www.nber.org/papers/w8156.

Kelley, C. (1997). Teacher compensation and organization. *Educational Evaluation and Policy Analysis, 19* (1), 15-28.

Kelley, C., & Odden, A. (1995). *Reinventing teacher compensation systems. CPRE Finance Brief.* Philadelphia, PA: Consortium for Policy Research in Education.

Klein, S. (1998). Standards for teacher tests. *Journal of Personnel Evaluation in Education, 12* (2), 123-138.

Koretz, D. (1996). Using student assessments for educational accountability. In E. A. Hanushek & D. W. Jorgenson (Eds.), *Improving America's schools: The role of incentives* (pp. 171-195). Washington, D.C.: National Research Council.

Larson, R. (1984). Teacher performance evaluation: What are the key elements? *NASSP Bulletin, 68* (469), 13-18.

Manzo, K. (1996, December 4). Vermont to combine standardized tests with portfolios. *Education Week.*

Meyer, R. (1997). Comments on chapters two, three and four. In H. Ladd (Ed.), *Holding Schools Accountable* (pp. 65 – 98) Washington, D.C.: Brookings Institution Press.

Meyers, R. (1996). Value-added indicators of school performance. In E. A. Hanushek & D. W. Joregenson (Eds.), *Improving America's schools: The role of incentives* (pp. 197-223). Washington, D.C.: National Academy Press.

Milanowski, A., Odden, A., & Youngs, P. (1998). Teacher knowledge and skill assessment and teacher compensation: An overview of measurement and linkage issues. *Journal of Personnel Evaluation in Education, 12* (2), 83-101.

Mitchell, Daniel J.B., David Lewin, and Edward E. Lawler (1990). "Alternative Pay Systems, Firm Performance, and Productivity." In Alan Blinder (Ed.), *Paying for Productivity: A Look at the Evidence.* Washington, DC: The Brookings Institution.

Mohrman, S. & Lawler, E. (1996). Motivation for school reform, In S. Fuhrman and J. O'Day (Eds.) *Rewards and Reform: Creating Educational incentives that Work*. Consortium for Policy Research and the Pew Forum on Education Reform. San Francisco: Jossey-Bass.

National Board for Professional Teaching Standards (2001). *National board certification process*. Available online at: http://www.nbpts.org/nat_board_certification/certification_process.html#assessment.

National Commission on Excellence in Education (1983). *A Nation at Risk.* Washington, D.C.: Author.

National Education Association (1999). *Frequently asked questions and answers regarding National Board Certification for NEA members.* www.nea.org/teaching/nbpts.

Odden, A. (2000, January). New and better forms of teacher compensation are possible. *Phi Delta Kappan, 81* (5), 361-366.

Odden, A. (n.d). *New and better forms of teacher compensation are possible.* Madison, WI: Consortium for Policy Research in Education, University of Wisconsin-Madison.

Pencavel, John (1977). "Work, Effort, On-the-Job Screening, and Alternative Methods of Remuneration." *Research in Labor Economics*, 1.

Peterson, K. (1988). Parent surveys for school teacher evaluation. *Journal of Personnel Evaluation in Education, 2,* 239-249.

Podgursky, M. (2001). Defrocking the National Board. Education Matters. Available online at http:www.educationnext.org.

Sanders, W., & Horn, S. (1998). Research findings from the Tennessee Value-Added Assessment System (TVAAS) database: Implications for educational evaluation and research. *Journal of Personal Evaluation in Education, 12* (3), 247-256.

Shanker, A. (1995). Where we stand: Beyond merit pay. Available online at http://www.aft.org/stand/previous/1995/011595.html.

Stronge, J. (1997). Improving schools through teacher education. In J. Stronge (Ed.), *Evaluating teaching. A guide to current thinking and best practice.* Thousand Oaks, CA: Corwin Press.

Stronge, J., & Ostrander, L. (1997). Client surveys in teacher evaluation. In J. Stronge (Ed.), *Evaluating teaching. A guide to current thinking and best practice*. Thousand Oaks, CA: Corwin Press.

Sullivan, C. (2000). *Into the classroom: Teacher preparation, licensure, and recruitment*. Alexandria, VA: National School Boards Association.

Viadero, D. (1993, November 10). RAND urges overhaul in Vermont's pioneering writing test. *Education Week, 1*, 18.

Webster, W. (1997). The connection between personnel evaluation and school evaluation. *Studies in Educational Evaluation, 21*, 227-254.

Weitzman, Martin L., and Douglas L. Kruse (1990). "Profit Sharing an Productivity." In Alan Blinder (Ed.), *Paying for Productivity: A Look at the Evidence.* Washington, DC: The Brookings Institution.

Wolf, K., Lichtenstein, G., Bartlett, E., & Hartman, D. (1996). Professional development and teaching portfolios: The Douglas County outstanding teacher program. *Journal of Personnel Evaluation in Education, 10*, 279-286.

# About the Author

Cheryl C. Sullivan, a former research analyst in NSBA's Policy Research Department, holds a Ph.D. from the University of Massachusetts-Amherst in the area of organizational behavior. Beyond this report and its companion monograph, *Into the Classroom: Teacher Preparation, Licensure, and Recruitment,* Cheryl is the author of several papers regarding effective recruitment strategies, promotion practices within professional service firms, and the efficacy of 360-degree personnel evaluation systems. She has taught managerial behavior and human resources at the University of Massachusetts-Amherst and George Mason University.

# About NSBA

The National School Boards Association is the nationwide organization representing public school governance. NSBA's mission is to foster excellence and equity in public elementary and secondary education through school board leadership. NSBA achieves its mission by representing the school board perspective before federal government agencies and with national organizations that affect education, and by providing vital information and services to state associations of school boards and local school boards throughout the nation.

NSBA advocates local school boards as the ultimate expression of grassroots democracy. NSBA supports the capacity of each school board—acting on behalf of and in close concert with the people of its community—to envision the future of education in its community, to establish a structure and environment that allow all students to reach their maximum potential, to provide accountability for the people of its community on performance in the schools, and to serve as the key community advocate for children and youth and their public schools.

Founded in 1940, NSBA is a not-for-profit federation of associations of school boards across the United States and its territories. NSBA represents the nation's 95,000 school board members that govern 14,890 local school districts serving the nation's more than 47 million public school students. Virtually all school board members are elected; the rest are appointed by elected officials.

NSBA policy is determined by a 150-member Delegate Assembly of local school board members. The 25-member Board of Directors translates this policy into action. Programs and services are administered by the NSBA executive director and a 150-person staff. NSBA is located in metropolitan Washington, D.C.

·NSBA·

National School Boards Association
1680 Duke Street
Alexandria, VA 22314-3493
Phone: 703-838-6722 • Fax: 703-683-7590

Web Address: *http://www.nsba.org* E-Mail: *info@nsba.org*
Excellence and Equity in Public Education through School Board Leadership